Battledore

New Women's Voices Series, No. 131

poems by

L.J. Sysko

Finishing Line Press
Georgetown, Kentucky

Battledore

New Women's Voices Series, No. 131

Copyright © 2017 by L.J. Sysko
ISBN 978-1-63534-214-7 First Edition
All rights reserved under International and Pan-American Copyright Conventions.
No part of this book may be reproduced in any manner whatsoever without written permission from the publisher, except in the case of brief quotations embodied in critical articles and reviews.

PUBLICATION CREDITS

Some of these poems appeared in journals. Thanks to the editors.

"Sitz Bath" in *Mom Egg Review*, vol. 14
"Checkout" in Amazon's *Day One*, April 28, 2014
"Just try" in *Best New Poets 2013*, ed. Brenda Shaughnessy
"Razor Cut" and "Ode to Botox" in *Sweetlit.com*, January 2013
"Waiting for someone who speaks" (previously published as "Pearlescent Omnivore") in *terrain.org*, October 1, 2012, Issue 30
"Spider Goat" in *5AM*, 2010
"Volcano" in *Ploughshares*, 2009, ed. Jean Valentine
"Motorcycle Ride" in *5AM*, 2009

Publisher: Leah Maines

Editor: Christen Kincaid

Cover Art: Laurie Hogin

Author Photo: Laura Novak

Cover Design: Elizabeth Maines McCleavy

Printed in the USA on acid-free paper.
Order online: www.finishinglinepress.com
          also available on amazon.com

Author inquiries and mail orders:
Finishing Line Press
P. O. Box 1626
Georgetown, Kentucky 40324
U. S. A.

Table of Contents

Checkout 1

Volcano 3

Sitz Bath 4

Mommy's Not Going Anywhere 6

Cupcake 7

Whim 8

Spider Goat 10

Waiting for someone who speaks 11

Battledore 13

Choose Your Own Adventure 15

Motorcycle Ride 17

Razor Cut 18

Drive-thru 20

Stream 21

Fierce Intelligence 22

Just try 23

Entitlement 26

Ode to Botox 27

Notes 29

"And now: it is easy to forget/ what I came for/among so many who have always/ lived here"
—Adrienne Rich, "Diving into the Wreck"

Checkout

Do you have a Loyalty card?
Cashier Guy smiles into his monitor,

ear gauge gaping—
fleshless slit. Like a vagina, lazing

in the sun between swims.
Little effacements fill your wallet,

promises to save you
money. They're not worth searching

for when you can type in coordinates.
Numbers tumble beneath us

as though we know our ocean's breadth.
How much time between continents?

Empathy's speed?
Ask Darwin's finches. They know:

isolation yields nothing
but mettle. Exhausted, one flies.

Refusing death's dull
drop into the sea,

she turns back, tear-blinded
to peck the Implacable open.

It yields. Sustenance reverberates,
calls another—.

Strangers nest together,
beginning again.

Old ways—rock-bashed,
tide-churned—sink

broken to the bottom.
Hunched between you,

a touch screen flickers.
Lascivious preener.

1s and 0s throw it open.
He slides a pen across the line.

Paper, white like a sail,
pen, a mast,

bear your hand across—
alone atop a swale.

Volcano

When the infant head bursts out,
the fire begins to die,
shoulders, like displaced rocks,
find a place to rest until they're pulled,
twisted out into the air to steam then cool.

Everything hisses and smokes
as when lava finds ocean.
Now, there's an After.
After it is done. After her first minute.
After they weigh, test, swaddle her.
After they hand her over
and she attacks the breast
like a castaway, found,
and given her first taste of water.

Ice chips, settled in their glass,
fall to the bottom,
like a floe after cataclysmic thaw.
Then, the giving tides of milk. Rising,
days and nights, rocking, rocking
on rolling seas of white.

Nowhere are there edges,
nothing but the constancy
of a familiar, unreachable horizon
see-sawing wildly in the distance
and the flowed lava,
like molasses chilled in a summer jar,
hardening to a stop underwater,
forming something new,
solid, and submerged.

Sitz Bath

You won't
lower your body
into this inch and a half

of lukewarm water.
Tectonic plates
have shifted,

unbraided until
a small volcanic island
hisses— steaming,

breathing in the distance.
No, you won't
pink this puddle

with your stitched perineum.
No, you won't
soak in an All-Clad turkey roaster

like your friend
whose bathtub refused to fill,
settling into it like a handled carcass.

You will rock
in this chair
on ice packs

and a wadded pad
and burn,
surge, and burn,

letting the lava run.
When you refuse the sitz bath's soothing,
when you ask him to fetch Preparation H,

tell him *don't admonish me.*
This is the new
topography, a small thorny vestige—

a jabbing rib
Adam won't ever
get back.

Mommy's Not Going Anywhere

She asks for pat-pats and you comply,
a series of circles and downward strokes,

First Mate sleepily swabbing the decks by night,
busy, even at this hour—

she dreams, twitching in distant silence,
breath lapping, slapping against you

like waves against a hull.

Cupcake

Muffins won't do
for little lichen kids—

>Valentines for the whole class,
>elves, fairies, seats cushioned in moss,
>gorse-legged desks, magnolia-veneered Mary Janes,
>reverse pleat loam, spore-stitched jumpers, acorn buttons,
>poison ivy pigtails, garter snakes halved, braided, and hanging.
>Blue jay yolks drunk, shells crushed black. Green Man debauched,
>dirty, drunk in the corner. Bat-wing bacchanal, tadpoles passing
>erect, fingering food, velvet wet, rabbit-multiplying at the back
>of night's moist maw.

From oven to cooling rack, you move.
Lightning stops
and things look simple.

Dawn rolls its blue body over to the light.
You spelunk upstairs to the nursery down the hall,
like a cave explorer   ducking past stalactites,
hearing   the drip   of close breath.

Whim

She dog ears the page:
>*I would write on the lintels of the doorpost, Whim.*

Questions flow across the
transom. Is it enough

to pencil a star in the margin?
Time beats, whining

sternum-hollow against her ear.
Heart, do you hear?

She's an arranger. Of things
in drawers and cradles, taking time

to polish and pluck, fold and toil.
She goes and comes

heedless through the door.
Like a puppy

bypassing his own leash for the cage,
you circle and circle

and sit down. Years pass that way—
husbands hewn, babies blown like glass

molten and magic in rooms below.
Your tail wags hard

against the floor, thwack THWACK.
My, you've been patient,

but, if she sticks that bone
through your slats again today,

will you finally growl? Will you
sniff it and turn away?

Or, will you close your eyes
and lick and lick until it yields

like taffy, sliding down your throat
to settle, sizzling into your system

while you nap.
In your dreams, your aging paw

scratches out *Whim*.
There, in drool, a new motto

blooms on your pillow:
        Whatever.

Spider Goat

The man at the podium says the FDA mulled it over because spider silk's stronger than Kevlar, the bullet-proof stuff, tensile strength and so on. When breast milk soaks your bra, you lose the thread of his lecture. Three years past the bra pad stage, but you feel the sizzle of let-down like butter sliding across a skillet. Spider goat the cause, the catalyst, and this bulgy white-haired man talking about Informatics and cloned wheat. And you suddenly have a problem, a problem you'd not had since the Produce aisle two years ago when someone else's baby began to wail from the cart next to the lettuce, and there you stood, wet in the bosom holding a Buddha hand. An alien fruit, perfumed, gnarled, new to you, and you'd been cradling it, a hand within a hand within the hand of America. You abandoned the cart and drove home, pulsing to a stop at the lights, outpacing everyone. As though you might outrun this indefatigable osmosis. In the closet, you peeled the bra and looked at your breasts, still there, still doing what they do, benignly resting like sages on the mount, like tortoises in the zoo who never move even if you stand there for what seems like forever to catch some sign, some inkling that they're animate. But they move when you're not watching. And the spider goat will awaken one day, having been a goat before she nodded off, to find she's being milked now in earnest. Something's given way. And it's sore. Spider silk swirls inside her mammary glands, courses through her—she's the eye of the needle, a poison dart, a flag staked in the furrow emblazoned with the word, *Theirs*.

Waiting for someone who speaks

to pull in the driveway
—breastfeeding,

pacing, rocking,
repeating, repeating,
repeating—

is to cringe down
like a toad between
mower blade and lawn

waiting it out.
Your skin,
pebbled pathos sensitized

like a chilled testicle enervating,
exposure pulling its taffy
tenderly close.

Your first croak,
its throaty gape,
null—such ballooning ceremony

for a bulbous fall.
Past and present choke
in the face of future's

rotors. Poor girl,
evolution's not caught up
to your larynx, your lyre.

He's here but deaf
anyway behind his machine,
and you've so much

to report, beginning,
beginning, beginning
with this—this intercession

in your garden.
Poison pools
behind your eyes—

weak substitute for story—.
Irony clouds your vision.
Can you stagger back, back,

back like a wounded
cowboy in a western—through
time's saloon doors to where

water warms you, where tadpoles
spawn, where eggs lap
against land's lip?

It's there, where song
could have been. Could we
slow time's rotors, reduce its

whooshing din? Could we?
Could we? Could we?

Battledore

The sun opens its mouth
to night, setting a curving

river aflame. You're there
swinging evening's pendulum.

It's ancient, your pounding—
battledore bearing down,

cloth heap dull and sodden,
body black, bending

like a tree rebuked by storm.
Stay your battledore, hold

your metronome silent.
Where river's fire burns darkest,

deeper than blue herons' careful
wading, you'll see reflections

shimmering: axman
striking, baseballer batting,

savage hunting, protester
picketing, politician

pontificating, striver
striving—.

History's insistent ones.
Did you see them? Were they

men? One epoch after
another, embattled

archetypes fledged against
you, snarling your mind's

gnarled roots, trapping you
shoal-shallow, even you—

you pugilist timekeeper.
You've pummeled a low

bassline for history's
winged thrash.

Choose Your Own Adventure

If you want Curmudgeon to love
Eep, stay right here,

keep reading please.
Look at the pictures.

See boneless Eep,
tiny, pink, and wild,

bounding around
corners, disappearing

behind the sharpest leaf.
He'll have to be brave

or foolhardy. We know
Curmudgeon won't do it.

He vacillates between casual cruelty
and passive sorcery,

black hat/white hat averaging out.
He's world-building

a grey ruin, harrumphing
his hang nail tender, chewing

tepid gerp, filling anxious buckets.
Gather your fleeceless moxie,

Eep! Discern danger from death,
squiggle this labyrinth straight,

show Curmudgeon how it's done,
propel us paragraph

by paragraph.
Some yell *Cowabunga!*

on their roads of trial.
But it's ok

if you close your eyes
and squeak, *Eep!*

It's what Curmudgeon loves best—
your hatless heroics, your somersault

across his transom, fevered and finished,
dropping onto his lap,

curling your tales
into yawning rings.

Your sleep.

Motorcycle Ride

Karaoke sessions in the Landolfi's basement, whirling atop the tiled *L* in the floor to *When Doves Cry,* trying to tag along. Doritos, Candies heels, Barbies, Cabbage Patch dolls, and Rick Springfield, and the day you rode on the back of Mr. Landolfi's new motorcycle, his Yamaha or Honda with its glittered blue finish, like a bowling ball split open and given wheels. You stood on the driveway's edge, looking past adults at chrome and pipes, moving slowly forward when asked if you wanted to go, then flying down the street, hands sweating, hair blowing, eyes fighting to stay open, to see it all go by—split levels and Colonials built in 1975, past brick and siding and swatches of lawn, then your house with its towering oak blurring past, whisked across a blacktop sea, you holding onto Mr. Landolfi's fat sides, his white t-shirt flapping, feeling the vibration between your legs, looking down then, shielding yourself from the wind on roads-once-horse-pastures, then the slow lean into the driveway, stillness feeling too still as you climbed off and somebody new took the seat.

Razor Cut

You're fomenting suburban rebellion
starting with your hair.

It began with Chemical Straightening
that crackled into brunette milli-shards

then the salvage: careful with a razor.
And so it's a kind of punk 'do,

disarray only undone by pillows.
Each morning, the back's resuscitated,

when hopeful fingers, elixirs coax the tortoise
from its shell. This must be what that hermit crab

felt like in 1988, when dad, wanting to verify
what the boardwalk sales-kid described

as a sick E.T. transitioning from a tight shell
to a roomier one, took pliers from the garage

and splintered then cracked it—
as though it were nothing

more than nutmeat to be turned over in our hands.
Let's see, he said. *It has to come out now.* And it did,

looking like E.T., hypothermic, translucent,
when it scooted forward once and died. A diminutive

Mercutio—*a plague! a plague!*, he might've eked out
if he'd not been voiceless, glass-boxed

in your suburban bedroom. It's tough
to say what the plague is.

Is it vanity—that drove you
to straighten already straight hair?

Is it incompetence
in the fuchsia-mohawked stylist

who backcombed what should've been left slack?
Or maybe it's this house, this life, so lucky

that leads you to tiptoe
onto the cold garage slab at night,

sweeping spider webs and WD-Forty aside,
looking for tools to crack it open.

Drive-thru

Your hide twitches—
Noah's ox

sitting between lion
and lamb,

feigning myopia.
Minivans idle in the drive-thru.

Baby in the back.
Beast in the mirror.

Stream

The soul, a fish in brackish water,
selects from what is visible,
what's nearest. From among murk and fronds,
she chooses mayflies, caddis flies, or mollusks—

across the bottom, she rakes.
Her shadow, trailing,
plinks a pebble free. Then she digs.
With indifference commensurate,
she deposits eggs and leaves.

Fierce Intelligence

When the brutish and dumb encamp far upriver
looking for weapons to wield, we'll enjoy their absence.
They'll return with cudgels in hand seeking our fire anyway.
Intelligence: application of logic and empathy to problems.

It doesn't need adjectival gunpowder.
But the fierce won't be vanquished
and the ignorant ride on their shoulders,
scaling battlements like spooky totems.

It's easier to let them in through the front door,
but then we'd have to live with them.
This storm season, let's huddle together
beneath the canopy, where ferns splash across bedrock,

peering dubious at nature's drawn curtain.
Whatever Happiness is, it listens
for silence at its waterfall door.
We'll wait for invitations in,

having howled ourselves hoarse,
deafened by soaked patience.
Inside, we'll be
hungry and sated,

flinty and fragile,
soft and keen,
delicate, abiding.
How will our tribe tell this story?—

After the deluge,
after we tuck our chins
and hold our breath, letting Paradise
drub our heads at the exit.

Just try

to crop out anachronisms—.

Power lines unzip your sunset
no matter how you wade

like an egret through
the salt marsh, bending at the waist,

primordial fronds and velvet
bulrushes smacking past your ears.

The camera's dumb eye captures
what we ask it to, entombing it

within its geometry.
In Photography 101,

your improbable pomegranate dusks
wouldn't reconcile

with what swam out of the developer's bath.
Where are Van Gogh's rollicking clouds?

Magritte's black and blue hour?
Your aftermath is so 4x6.

The fault is yours.
You're sure of it. It's the way you talk

without looking at him.
It's the way you struggle

against anger. It's the way our heroes slow
and sicken. It's the way it's presented

in the news. There's so much to be sad about.
You'd rather look away. But you're telling yourself

to be careful. Be careful about disparity,
about contrast, about separation. You're saying

no to the phone gripped assiduously
in doctors' waiting rooms. In the chairs

someone's lined up like boats in a marina,
you force your eyes up to ask

an old question: why should you be
a me, a fisherman, or anyone? We leave

fingerprints on our photos, our screens,
the sliding windows that divide us.

You park your car—idle, with its
hazards on, hood half in the cattails,

pointing to the scallop boats' dock, where
men smoke and gather, laughing,

acting cavalier like bored knights,
steering fork lifts one-handed,

piling ice chests for tonight's deep sea
charter. Even if the power plant's reactors

pepper your horizon, you wade deeper
for a picture. A Herring Gull

drops a Blue Crab then lands
to peck its pale underbelly open.

Feathers and shell white as the sky,
sure as the tide, invite more gulls to land.

Their eyes blink
and blink in time with yours.

Entitlement

Americasaurus Rex ate the moon.
Stars dangle from its maw like fronds
chewed to make the pill go down,
but cataclysm's coming, flying fast
with destruction packed on its back
like a hobo's bindle. So before
throngs flee the theatre yelling *Zowie*
or *Yikes* with 3D glasses
impeding their progress to what's bound
to be a locked exit anyway, let's sit back down
for some home movies. Every family
winds this wheel together,
lurching down time's tracks.

We tell our stories in the dark, tongues returning
to loss, feeling along a sore tooth's topography—
nimble like an elephant's trunk—smiling
despite the wadded poultice packed
against our gums. Like candy beached inside
a molar atoll, entitlement's a dissolving patch.
It might hurt later, but suckle it anyway.
Savor it while it lasts, but don't
be surprised when the lights come up
and the place looks looted.

Ode to Botox

When the vial thrums and throbs
a needle to dripping life,

they hum, keeping time for the coming alchemy:
Big Bang in the doctor's office,

lightning and bacteria in a bottle,
cc's of creation piercing the skin,

planets colliding, ether parting,
the bands swaddling the Cosmos tight

relaxing, softening. Sigh—can you feel it?
See the world where it started.

Liquidy and hot, temperate, tropical,
a Paleolithic sauna. It's tough to be angry

when it's so comfortable.
And that's how fighting would stop,

justice return—to water.
90% water at birth, they say,

and you've acknowledged it, letting primordial
pools swell, swirling what's poison and plenty

behind your countenance.
You are a woman underwater so let its

peace buffet you— its ruinous tides,
indecorous currents. Take your hands

and let them do the work. But your face?
Grant it medically assisted paralysis.

There is a return, a womb
that will carry us again: Clostridium botulinum.

So walk in vanity because it's not vanity at all,
not in the way it sounds, but in the way it looks,

like truth restored, like Eve when she was just Eve—no apple,
no snake, no man, no kids, no minivan. Go ahead,

don't let them make you feel bad about it. You are
water and toxin, balm and danger, modern and very, very old.

Notes

"Battledore": A battledore or beetle was a wooden bat used throughout history as part of the laundering process. Women—at riverside, in washhouses, or in tubs— pounded linens to agitate dirt out of textiles.

"Drive-thru" alludes to Edward Hicks' painting *Peaceable Kingdom* (1826), part of the permanent collection of The Philadelphia Museum of Art. Hicks, an Early American Folk painter, expressed Quaker ideals through his work, rendering similar subjects 61 times during his career and titling them all identically. In the compositions, animals and children coexist peaceably and idyllically, alluding to the Biblical story of Isaiah (11:6-8 and 65:25).

"Just try": The "old question" referenced in this poem is that asked by Elizabeth Bishop in her poem "In the Waiting Room." The faithful quotation is: "Why should I be my aunt,/ or me, or anyone?"

"Motorcycle Ride" was written in deference to Gerald Stern's "The Dancing."

"Spider Goat": To generate a reliable volume of strong "spider silk," scientists at The University of Wyoming injected goats with spider genes; the goats' silk protein-supplemented milk could then be synthesized for industrial and military uses, such as in production of bulletproof vests. Content taken from a speech given in 2010 by Dr. Andrew C. von Eschenbach.

"Stream" alludes to Emily Dickinson's poem "The Soul selects her own Society."

"Whim" includes a quotation from Ralph Waldo Emerson's *Self-Reliance*. "I would write on the lintels of the doorpost, Whim" comes from that work.

Acknowledgments

First, let me thank my family.

Ryan, Siena, and Reeve, we form a circle around our family's fire—and the occasional blue glow of my laptop. You have made a life for me in which both words and love abound. I love you!

Mom and Dad, thank you for feeding me books, providing for my education, and teaching me how valuable my voice is. Your voices are here, too.

Thanks to Nana and Poppop; your resilient optimism founded a family of talkers and teachers.

Grants from Delaware Division of the Arts have been welcome gifts as have funds from Tower Hill School for conferences and workshops.

I appreciate Laurie Hogin's generosity. The cover image is one of her amazing paintings: "Home Fires, 8 of 13," Oil on panel with artist-made frame, 2011. Courtesy of the artist and Littlejohn Contemporary, New York. To see more of her work, visit lauriehogin.com.

A heartfelt thanks goes to all of my teachers from Pennsbury School District to The Lawrenceville School to Lafayette College to New England College and on to the finest teachers of all, my own students.

Anne Marie Macari, Paula McLain, and Lee Upton, thank you for showing me that permission isn't necessary and language has body.

About the Poet

L.J. Sysko is a poet and writer whose work has appeared in *Best New Poets 2013, Ploughshares, Day One, Rattle, 5am,* and other journals. She holds an MFA in Poetry from New England College. She has been the recipient of both an Emerging Artist's grant and an Opportunity grant from the Delaware Division of the Arts; other honors include the Academy of American Poets' Jean Corrie Prize, Lafayette College's H. MacKnight Black Prize, and three awards from the Dorothy Sargent Rosenberg Memorial Foundation. Proud to have her work appear as part of Finishing Line Press' New Women's Voices Series, Sysko teaches high school English and lives with her husband and two children. For more information, visit ljsysko.com.

www.ingramcontent.com/pod-product-compliance
Lightning Source LLC
LaVergne TN
LVHW041506070426
835507LV00012B/1357